I0499803

Emerging new India
2019-2024

Compiled, Written & Published By :

Aditya Kumar Daga

3C Gopi Bose Lane, First Floor, Kolkata-700012

Phone :- +919432221255

Email : adityadaga25@yahoo.com

First Edition

© No part of this publication including any Heading, Style, Graph or Statistics can be used or reproduced in any form online or offline or by any means or translation in any other language without the express permission in writing of Aditya Kumar Daga as well

No person can export this book online or offline except with the express permission of Aditya Kumar Daga the Writer and Publisher of This Book.

Printed and Marketed By

KDP Amazon

Caution Note

I have tried my best to compile the data from the most reliable sources of the Government.

This Book is to encourage Students, youngsters, entrepreneurs lacking proper knowledge under one roof.

This Book is my genuine effort to provide the correct guideline to every-one interested seriously to do something big.

However 'to err is human' and I am no more an exception. I might do lot of mistakes here. So please recheck.

Before setting up any skill or machine oriented industry please cross-check everything twice and plan thrice.

Writer & Publisher & Printers are in no way responsible for any failure or damages or pull back on anyone's part.

My sole aim is to provide a proper guideline under one roof to pace the commercial & industrial work smoothly.

All data & statistics, declarations, Govt. Policies, Estimates have been compiled from varied general public sources.

I wish all the patron to move cautiously with a hope of best of the time ahead.

This book is a compilation of Data from different sources for the benefit of mass and give or sold at the cost of bringing this book to the people

Preface

Despite so many incentives provided by the State & Central Government to set up an Industry; so many reforms made to ease the procedures of providing Licenses, Approvals, Clearances, No objection etc.; removal of so many hurdles related to Allowances/ Grant of permission of electricity, water & other infrastructural facilities there is no substantial improvement in the Industrial Growth Rate. The reason behind it: -

Unawareness on the part of new investors specially our Youth and new Entrepreneurs regarding the facilities provided by the Govt. and procedures of seeking such facilities.

Moreover there is a wide-spread ignorance among investors regarding where & how they should collect proper information's to start with and how to summaries available information if any to set up a project. Even though there is a vast pool of information's available through different sources but of little use if such sources could not be tapped by the investors.

Till date no "Website" or "Book" is available which can guide the Investors step by step to begin "to set up an Industry" or "to choose one option out of so many option regarding choosing up of Land, Products, etc.

During the time of our project execution in last 15 years MCPL has come across the basic problem with most of the investors that they can not come to any decision out of so many alternatives related to selection of an industry, selection of a product, selection of Land, selection of Equity Pattern, Collaboration/Technology etc. And being set into a mess of so many raw information most of investors either turned down their proposals and if carried on then waste a huge amount of money at the initial stage of Project set up.

So this is the first attempt of MCPL to guide such Investors "HOW TO SELECT AN OPPURTUNITY." This book is more emphasizing in How, Where, When & Why you should choose a project so that you could easily determine over one product/industry/location.

I hope that my attempt to provide logical guideline would be appreciated by you.

Regards

Aditya Kumr Daga

Before we go to the detail discussions about the "WHERE, HOW, WHEN & WHY UNIT SHOULD BE SET UP" we should know: -

INDIA IS the 7th largest , 2nd most populous country and largest democracy in the world. The far reaching and sweeping economic reforms undertaken since 1991 have unleashed the enormous growth potential of economy. There have been a rapid move towards deregulation and liberalization as a result of which India becomes the one of the most Developing Countries as well as a hot destination for investment of the world.

One of the largest economies of the world, fourth largest economy in terms of purchasing power parity.

Large & rapidly growing consumer market-up to 300 million people constitute the market for branded consumer products.

Easy access to markets of the other nations belong to SAARC

Large & Diversified infrastructure spread across the country.

Well developed research & development infrastructure and technical activities.

Abundance of natural resources and agricultural self sufficiency.

Developed banking system, commercial banking network of over 63,000 branches supported by a number of national and state-level financial institutions.

Vibrant capital market, consisting of 22 stock exchanges with over 9,000 listed companies.

Skilled manpower and professional management including engineers, managerial personnel, accountants and lawyers available at competitive costs.

Conducive foreign investment environment that provides freedom of entry, investment, location, choice of technology, production of repatriation of capital, dividends etc.

Well balanced package of fiscal incentives.

Established independent judiciary.

English the preferred business language.

Despite of having such a good atmosphere for development of industries the graph of the substantial growth of industries is not satisfactory. It is because in India there is lack of nodal agency which can provide proper logical and complete guidelines to any new investor or present promoter to decide upon a particular project to be set up out of several alternatives considering the

Location Factors
Subsidy, Incentive & Fund Involvement Factors
Export, Import & Re-export Probability Factors
Procedural Difficulties Factor
Upcoming Government Circulars On Legal, Commercial, Financial, Economic Matters

promoter is always in doldrums or in confusion what is the best alternative to be accepted or the best approach, location or category of the project to be adopted to cover full opportunity cost & enjoy the complete economy of scale.

Further a new investor or a present promoter (in case of diversification) does not know: -

WHAT protection he will get from Govt. or any other autonomous agencies & **HOW** he should get the protection.

WHAT protection he may get in case of import liberalization of various product in the same class or category giving very tough marketing condition and **HOW** he should get the protection.

WHAT protection he is getting in case of labor unrest, in case of labor intensive unit or power problem in case of any capital-intensive unit and **HOW** he should get the protection.

WHAT protection he should get to curve in case of new policies regarding export barriers, export rejection or in case of financial instability in the Global market and **HOW** he should get the protection.

WHAT protection he may enjoy in case of WTO Free Trade Policies in between the number of countries or regarding patent or trademark registration under the GATT policies.

WHAT protection, prevention and cure he might be having in case of premature collaboration failure & **HOW** he should get compensate these failures.

WHAT protection he should get regarding smooth supply of Raw material from country or abroad as well as marketing with guaranteed payment.

We are hereby trying our level best to guide a promoter to set up a new **PROJECT or EXPAND & DIVERSIFY THE PRESENT ACTIVITIES** so that they could follow logical step

We are hereby trying our level best to guide a promoter to set up a new **PROJECT or EXPAND & DIVERSIFY THE PRESENT ACTIVITIES** so that they could follow logical step

> **To Decide Upon "A PARTICULAR PROJECT"**

Whether in Service Sector
Whether in Infrastructure Sector
Whether in Industrial Items
Whether in Consumer Items

> **To Set Up Under "A PARTICULAR CATEGORY"**

Export promotion projects
Export oriented Projects
100% export Projects
Ancillary Units
Small Scale Industry projects

> **in "A PARTICULAR LOCATION"**

Export processing Zone.
Special economic Zone.
Industrial Parks.
Industrial Growth Centres.
Industrial Estates.
Any General Area(On Freehold or Rented)

Which could be at best, managed in the investment capacity of the promoter and fund syndication probability of the financial institutions.

In this book we will discuss in detail about the **In what, Where, Why & How a promoter should choose a project.**

What ?

what ??? *Men, Money, Material And Machines* are essential to set up an unit but more essential than these is promoter's decision about to what sort of unit and in which category do you want to set up.

In this chapter we are trying to help you to select an Unit. **What** is to be produced is the most difficult and a sensitive task for the New Promoters rather than the experienced Businessmen. Project can be categorised in so many ways: -

As per nature of product (like consumer product/ industrial product/ service oriented product)

As per joint venture project (collaboration project, ancillaries, subsidiary Project)

As per Raw Material oriented project (i.e. Food processing, Horticulture, Floriculture etc)

As per labor intensive/ capital intensive project

Thus **"PROJECT & PRODUCT IDENTIFICATION" IS THE MOST VITAL PART OF THE PROJECT WHICH SHOULD BE DONE VERY CAREFULLY**

According to our experience it was seen that investors with capacity of investment go on searching numerous projects with no results ultimately.

At FIRST Investors must analyze their <u>OWN PRIORITIES</u> related to projects as per their experience, interest and ambition/dreams as well as their preliminary study. They should not take fancy for a particular line merely because some of their known person has made enormous profit or have attained social status through a particular industry. It is to be noted that If proper & organized study be made on a few projects only considering the following factors then decision will be more fruitful & time worthy

Promoters' previous experience and interest.

Present thrust areas in projects as declared by different agencies.

Present national and international trade and industry policies of the Government.

Present Incentive Policies of the Central & State Govt.

Present Global Trade Treaties with different countries.

Present Import Substituted Projects and Products.

Present Export Promoted or Oriented Projects and Products.

Present Collaboration available in term of Technology, Marketing & Equity.

Minimum promoter's contribution (which is around 35-40 % of the Project Cost.

Present facilities of Raw Material sourcing.

Present facilities of marketing and outsourcing.

Present facilities of exporting of product and importing of Raw material.

Finally Project Pay-Back Period & Viability Factor .

Quality of project –whether Import substituted; Export oriented or promoted; Ancillary Projects; New Global Concept projects.

After studying about the above points one by one and choosing projects go through the following tests:

The **preliminary** and process of the product should not take too long time in case of a manufacturing unit.

Avoid the Projects, which are in the negative list of the Government Policies.

Avoid much more technical complicacies so that work should continue smoothly.

Demand for the product should be sustained and erratic.

Whether project could have scope for future expansion
The product has little competition

The return on investment should be quick. Care must be taken towards the position of cash liquidity.

Procurement of machinery and raw materials should not pose big problems.

Technical & skilled persons should be easily available.

Better it has export prospects as nowadays Govt. has taken more thrust in export.

After selecting few projects promoter should begin detailed study considering the above said factors one by one.

Getting consensus over two to three projects, study should be made again over the Market-Feasibility, Project-Cost, Promoters Margin, Pay-back Period, Financial Feasibility etc. for each project.

Out of these promoters could make a few studies themselves through internet or marketing Pioneers or Govt. agencies and official records. The addresses of few of them are given at the end of our book.

However to shape the above tasks into a proper study and to arrive at a proper decision, all the datas should be brought in Black and White called as DETAILED PROJECT FEASIBILITY REPORT where promoters will get all the details regarding Pay-Back Period, Break-Even, NRR, Financial viability etc.

Medleys Consortium Pvt. Ltd.(MCPL) based in Kolkata provides all sorts of Support Services in this regard.

India is on the threshold of major reforms and is poised to become the third-largest economy of the world by 2030. In the words of our Humble Prime Minister, India offers the 3 'Ds' for business to thrive— democracy, demography and demand. Add to that a tech-savvy and educated population, skilled labor, robust legal and IPR regime, and a strong commitment to calibrated liberalization — India is a destination that German investors cannot overlook. India's manufacturing sector has evolved through several phases - from the initial industrialization and the license raj to liberalization and the current phase of global competitiveness. Today, Indian manufacturing companies in several sectors are targeting global markets and are becoming formidable global competitors. Many are already amongst the most competitive in their sectors.

DEMOGRAPHICS ADVANTAGE:

The country is expected to rank amongst the world's top three growth economies and amongst the top three manufacturing destinations by 2020.

Favorable demographic dividends for the next 2-3 decades. Sustained availability of quality workforce.

Strong consumerism in the domestic market.

Strong technical and engineering capabilities backed by top-notch scientific and technical institutes.

The cost of manpower is relatively low as compared to other countries.

INFRASTRUCTURE:

Industrial Parks: Every state in India has developed industrial parks for setting up of industries.

National Investment & Manufacturing Zones: NIMZ is a combination of production units, public utilities, logistics, residential areas and administrative services. It would have a processing area, where manufacturing facilities, along with associated logistics and other services and required infrastructure will be located, and a non-processing area, to include residential, commercial and other social and institutional infrastructure.

Special Economic Zones: India has also developed SEZs that are specifically delineated enclaves treated as foreign territory for the purpose of industrial, service and trade operations, with relaxation in customs duties and a more liberal regime in respect of other levies, foreign investment. Sector specific clusters: like electronic manufacturing clusters, mega food parks etc: The government of India has been promoting the development of sector specific parks.

Country specific zones: The country also have few dedicated zones for industrial units from countries for example Neemrana Japanese Zone etc.

Industrial corridors: The Government of India is developing the Delhi-Mumbai Industrial Corridor (DMIC) as a global manufacturing and investment destination utilizing the 1,483 km-long, high-capacity western Dedicated Railway Freight Corridor (DFC) as the backbone. The objective is to increase the share of manufacturing in the GDP of the country and to create smart sustainable cities where manufacturing will be the key economic driver.

Other four corridors: planned include Bangalore Mumbai Economic Corridor (BMEC); Amritsar - Kolkata Industrial Development Corridor (AKIC); Chennai Bangalore Industrial Corridor (CBIC), East Coast Economic Corridor (ECEC) with Chennai Vizag Industrial Corridor as the first phase of the project (CVIC).

INCENTIVES OFFERED FOR MANUFACTURING:

Sector specific initiatives: The government of India provides sector specific subsidies for promoting manufacturing for example in order to boost manufacturing of electronics, the Govt. of India provides capital subsidy of up to 25% for 10 years.

Area based incentives: Incentives are provided for units in SEZ/NIMZ as specified in respective acts or setting up project in special areas like North East Region, Jammu & Kashmir, and Himachal Pradesh & Uttarakhand.

Incentives under income tax act:

Investment Allowance: The Government of India in its Union Budget 2014-15, has provided investment allowance at the rate of 15 per cent to a manufacturing company that invests more than US$ 4.17 million in any year in new plant and machinery.

Deductions: Several additional deductions are provided for instance deduction equal to 30% of additional wages paid to new regular workmen employed by the assesses over and above 50 workmen.

R&D Incentives: Higher weighted deductions of 200% provided for expenditure related to R&D subject to fulfilment of conditions.

Export Incentives: Under the foreign trade policy exports have been provided with several incentives like duty drawback, duty remission schemes etc.

State Incentives: Apart from above each state in India offers additional incentives for industrial projects. Some of the states also have separate policies for textile sector.

Incentives are in areas like rebated land cost; relaxation in stamp duty exemption on sale/lease of land;

Power tariff incentives; concessional rate of interest on loans; investment subsidies / tax incentives; backward areas subsidies; special incentive packages for mega projects.

RECENT INITIATIVES & BUDGET ANNOUNCEMENTS FOR PROMOTING MANUFACTURING:

The corporate tax rate for companies registered in India to go down from 30% to 25% of net profits in a phased manner over the next four years starting from FY 16-17.

An expert committee to examine the possibility and prepare a draft legislation where the need for multiple prior permission can be replaced by a pre-existing regulatory mechanism.

Goods and Services Tax proposed to be implemented from April 01, 2016.

The process of applying for Industrial License (IL) and Industrial Entrepreneur Memorandum (IEM) has been made online.

Initial validity period of Industrial License has been increased to three years from two years, also, two extensions of two years each in the initial validity of three years of the Industrial License shall now be allowed up to seven years. This will give enough time to licensees to procure land and obtain the necessary clearances/approvals from authorities.

Operational zing the e-BIZ portal: Through eBiz portal, a business user can fill the eForms online/offline, upload the attachments, make payment online and submit the forms for processing of the department.

Labor reforms: A dedicated Shram Suvidha Portal: The portal would allot Labor Identification Number (LIN) to nearly 6 lakhs units and allow them to file online compliance for 16 out of 44 labor laws

An all-new Random Inspection Scheme: Utilizing technology to eliminate human discretion in selection of units for Inspection, and uploading of Inspection Reports within 72 hours of inspection mandatory

Universal Account Number: Enables 4.17 crore employees to have their Provident Fund account portable, hassle-free and universally accessible

Apprentice Protsahan Yojana: Will support manufacturing units mainly and other establishments by reimbursing 50% of the stipend paid to apprentices during first two years of their training

Department of Industrial Policy and Promotion has identified various areas and action points on ease of doing business index/indicators have been prepared for assessing the overall business performance of the country as well as States/Union Territories.

Government has undertaken a number of steps to improve Ease of Doing Business in India. A large number of components of Defence Products' list have been excluded from the purview of Industrial Licensing. The application process for Industrial License and Industrial Entrepreneur's Memorandum has been made easy by simplification of form and making the process online 24X7. The validity period of the Industrial License and security clearance from Ministry of Home Affairs has been increased. The process of registration with Employees' Provident Fund Organization and Employees' State Insurance Corporation has been made on line and real-time. Process of obtaining environment and forest clearances has been made online. The Department of Industrial Policy and Promotion has advised Ministries and State Governments to simplify and rationalize the regulatory environment through business process reengineering and use of information technology. 14 Government of India services have been integrated with the online single window eBiz portal

SKILL INDIA: a multi-skill development programme has been initiated with a mission for job creation and entrepreneurship for all socio-economic classes. It endeavors to establish an international equivalent of the Indian framework on skill development, creating workforce mobility and enhancing youth employability.

SECTOR OPPORTUNITIES: INDIA PROVIDES GREAT AVENUES FOR INVESTMENTS IN VARIOUS SECTORS.

Defense: India is expected to spend US$ 40 billion on defense purchases over the next 4-5 years. The opening of the strategic defense sector for private sector participation will help foreign original equipment manufacturers to enter into strategic partnerships with Indian companies and leverage the domestic markets and also aim at global business.

Automotive: India is expected to become a major automobile manufacturing hub and the third largest market for automobiles by 2020, according to a report published by Deloitte. India is currently the seventh-largest automobiles producer in the world with an average annual production of 17.5 million vehicles, and is on way to become the fourth largest automotive market by volume, by 2015.

Engineering: The Indian Engineering sector has witnessed a remarkable growth over the last few years driven by increased investments in infrastructure and industrial production. The engineering sector, being closely associated with the manufacturing and infrastructure sectors of the economy, is of strategic importance to India's economy. Growth in the sector is driven by various sub-sectors such as infrastructure, power, steel, automotives, oil & gas, consumer durables etc.

Textiles: The Indian textiles industry, currently estimated at around US $108 billion, is expected to reach US $ 141 billion by 2021. The Indian textile industry has the potential to grow five-fold over the next ten years to touch US$ 500 billion mark on the back of growing demand for polyester fabric, according to a study by Wazir Advisors and PCI Xylenes and Polyester. The US$ 500 billion market figure consists of domestic sales of US$ 315 billion and exports of US$ 185 billion.

Chemicals: The Indian chemical industry stands as the third largest producer in Asia and 12th in world, in terms of volume. This industry could grow at 14 per cent per annum to reach a size of US$ 350 billion by 2021. India accounts for approximately 7 per cent of the world production of dyestuff and dye intermediates and is currently the world's third largest consumer of polymers and fourth largest producer of agrochemicals.

Food Processing: The Indian food industry stood around (US$ 39.03 billion) in 2013 and is expected to grow at a rate of 11 per cent to touch (US$ 64.31 billion) by 2018.

Leather: India's leather industry has witnessed robust growth, transforming from a mere raw material supplier to a value-added product exporter. In fact, today, almost 50 per cent of India's leather business comes from international trade.

Pharmaceuticals: The Indian pharmaceutical industry is estimated to grow at 20 per cent compound annual growth rate (CAGR) over the next five years, as per India Ratings, a Fitch Group company. Indian pharmaceutical manufacturing facilities registered with US Food and Drug Administration (FDA) as on March 2014 was the highest at 523 for any country outside the US. We expect the domestic pharma market to grow at 10-12 per cent in FY15 as compared to 9 per cent in FY14, as per a recent report from Centrum Broking. The domestic pharma growth rate was 11.9 per cent in October 2014, high-lighted the report.

Electronics: The electronics market is one of the largest in the world and is anticipated to reach US$ 400 billion in 2022 from US$ 69.6 billion in 2012. The market is pro-jected to grow at a compound annual growth rate (CAGR) of 24.4 per cent during 2012-2020.

ELECTRONICS SYSTEMS DESIGN & MANUFACTURING

Heavy industries

Machineries

Engines

Tools

Steel products

Industrial equipment's

Electrical and Home Appliances

Builders Hardware

Railway and related products and equipment's

The Indian electronics system design and manufacturing (ESDM) industry is at a huge inflection point. From being predominantly consumption driven, the Indian ESDM industry has a major potential to become a design led manufacturing industry. The industry is one of the fastest growing sectors in the country. The Indian ESDM industry was estimated to be $68.31 billion in 2012. The impressive guidance between 2011 and 2015 for this industry is expected to result in a Compound Annual Growth Rate (CAGR) of 9.88 percent. The corresponding size of the industry by 2015 is anticipated to be $94.2 billion. Reasons to Invest

Huge consumption market: The corresponding size of the industry by 2015 is anticipated to be $94.2 billion. Large demand to be generated due to government schemes like the National Knowledge Network (NKN), National Optical Fibre Network (NOFN), tablets for the Education sector, a digitisation policy and various other broadband schemes.

Attractive Incentives: The central and state government have announced scheme of incentives for manufacturing of electronics. Incentives include up to 25% capital subsidy on capital expenditure, giving land at rebated cost, reimbursement of central and state duties, income tax exemptions on setting up in special economic zones, assistance in skill development etc.

Availability of the infrastructure: The government is promoting development of electronics manufacturing clusters throughout the country to provide world class infrastructure and facilities. The Government of India has also received the applications of two consortia (IBM, Jaypee Group, Tower Jazz; ST Microelectronics, HSMC) to establish 2 semiconductor wafer fabrication units in Gujarat and Noida with the aim of operating at 20 nm process node within two years of initial operations and reaching a capacity of at least 40,000 WSPM of at least 300 mm size.

Availability of Skilled Manpower: India has the third largest pool of scientists and technicians in the world. Skilled manpower is available in abundance in Semiconductor Design and Embedded Software. India also has strong design and R&D capabilities in auto electronics and industrial electronics.

Investment Opportunities:

Setting up of Electronics Manufacturing Clusters.

Semiconductor Wafer Fabrication (FAB).

Electronic products like telecom equipment, LED's, consumer electronics, medical electronics, automotive electronics etc.

Electronic Components.

Semiconductor Design.

Electronics Manufacturing Services (EMS).

Defense Indian defense sector is at the cusp of an inflexion point wherein the future growth will be propelled by indigenous manufacturing both for domestic & global clients. The sector will witness strong growth over the next decade due to its current size, longevity, and competitive advantages. As per FICCI-Centrum report the market opportunity for Indian companies (PSU + Pvt) will grow 7x from $6bn in FY14 to $41bn by FY22. Reasons to Invest

India has some of the basic ingredients (large and relatively low cost (Frugal) engineering talent pool, comfort of western nations with India from a geo-political perspective) to exploit this opportunity but it will have to significantly improve on some others (technology, lack of a defence manufacturing ecosystem, etc). Also, the nature of warfare is becoming more software intensive, which plays into the strength of India considering IT sector growth in the past two decades.

India may become a large sourcing base for components and sub-systems in the years to come for foreign systems integrators this will happen as these companies face price pressure in the years ahead as the large arms consumers – US and the western developed world – seek cut backs on defense spending to improve their financial position and rein in fiscal deficits and debt/GDP ratios. Already a number of JVs have been signed between Indian and foreign players.

The offset clause (which stipulates that 30-50% of the armament purchase value should be spent on buying Indian components, sub-systems and products) introduced in capital purchase agreements with foreign defence players will ensure that an ecosystem of suppliers is built domestically.

Indigenization will take centre stage and gather pace going forward. Government has taken a number of steps in this direction. DPP 2013 furthers the cause of developing domestic defence sector by prioritizing procurement from Indian companies and buying from global companies as the last resort.

Recent Government Initiatives:

53% of the defence items for manufacturing by private sector have been de-licensed and dual use items having military as well as civilian applications if not specifically mentioned deregulated.

FDI cap raised to 49% and beyond 49% wherever it is likely to result in access to modern and 'state-of-art' technology in the country. The procurement process would be made more efficient, time bound and predictable so that the industry can plan its investment and R & D well in advance to meet the requirement of our armed forces.

Streamlining procedure in case of defense exports. There is a big opportunity in the defense sector for both domestic and foreign investors. We have the third largest armed force in the world with an annual budget of about US$ 38 billion and 40% of this is used for capital acquisition. In the next 7-8 years, we would be investing more than US 130 billion in modernization of our armed forces.

AUTOMOBILES

Demographically and economically, India's automotive industry is well-positioned for growth, servicing both domestic demand and, increasingly, export opportunities. A predicted increase in India's working-age population is likely to help stimulate the burgeoning market for private vehicles. Rising prosperity, easier access to finance and increasing affordability is expected to see four-wheelers gaining volumes, although two wheelers will remain the primary choice for the majority of purchasers, buoyed by greater appetite from rural areas, the youth market and women. Reasons to Invest:

Over the next 20 years, India will be a part of the big global automotive triumvirate.

Growth factors - growth in demand on back of rising income, expanding middle class and young population base, large pool of skilled manpower and growing technology; The country enjoys natural advantage and is among the lowest cost producers of steel in the world.

Tractor sales in the country are expected to grow at CAGR of 8-9% in the next five years, upping India's market potential for international brands.

Two-wheeler production has grown from 8.5 Million units annually to 15.9 Million units in the last seven years. Significant opportunities exist in rural markets.

India's car market has the potential to grow to 6+ Millions units annually by 2020.

The emergence of large automotive clusters in the country: Delhi-Gurgaon-Faridabad in the north, Mumbai-Pune-Nashik- Aurangabad in the west, Chennai-Bengaluru-Hosur in the south and Jamshedpur-Kolkata in the east. '

Global car majors have been ramping up investments in India to cater to growing domestic demand. These manufacturers plan to leverage India's competitive advantage to set up export-oriented production hubs.

An R&D hub: strong support from the government in the setting up of NATRiP centres. Private players such as Hyundai, Suzuki, GM are keen to set up an R&D base in India.

Tata Nano is a sterling example of Indian frugal engineering and is being positioned as a mobilizer of the young generation.

Electric cars are likely to be a sizeable market segment in the coming decade.

Multinational automotive plants in India rank among the top across the world in terms of their productivity and quality.

Largest tractor manufacturer; 2nd largest two wheeler manufacturer; 2nd largest bus manufacturer; 5th largest heavy truck manufacturer; 6th largest car manufacturer; 8th largest commercial vehicle manufacturer.

Investment Opportunities:

Two-wheelers (motorcycles, geared and ungeared scooters and mopeds),

Three wheelers,

Commercial vehicles (light, medium and heavy),

Passenger cars,

Utility vehicles (UVs) and Tractors.

Production in 2013-14 – Passenger vehicles – 3.1 million; two wheelers – 16.9 million; commercial vehicles – 0.7 million; three wheelers – 0.8 million increasing every year by around 12-14% in Peak seasons .

ENGINEERING

The Indian Engineering sector has witnessed a remarkable growth over the last few years driven by increased investments in infrastructure and industrial production. The engineering sector, being closely associated with the manufacturing and infrastructure sectors of the economy, is of strategic importance to India's economy. Growth in the sector is driven by various sub-sectors such as infrastructure, power, steel, automotives, oil & gas, consumer durables etc. The country now joins an exclusive group of 17 countries who are permanent signatories of the WA, an elite international agreement on engineering studies and mobility of engineers. Reasons to Invest:

The engineering sector in India attracts immense interest from foreign players as it enjoys a comparative advantage in terms of manufacturing costs, technology and innovation.

Capacity creation in sectors such as infrastructure, power, mining, oil & gas, refinery, steel, automotive, and consumer durables driving demand in the engineering sector.

The government has an ambitious mission of 'Power for all by 2012' and has planned capacity additions of 120 GW in the 12th Five-Year Plan.

Governmental infrastructure projects such as Golden Quadrilateral and the North-South and East-West corridors fuelled growth in the engineering sector

India has Comparative advantage vis-à-vis peers in terms of manufacturing costs, market knowledge, technology and creativity.

More than 2,500 firms in the engineering sector have ISO 9000 accreditation.

The engineering sector is a growing market. Current spending on engineering services is projected to increase to US$ 1.1 trillion by 2020.

The Indian engineering sector is of strategic importance to the economy owing to its intense integration with other industry segments. The sector has been de-licensed and enjoys 100 per cent FDI. With the aim to boost the manufacturing sector it has announced scheme for capital goods sector.

Engineering exports from India are expected to cross US$ 70 billion in FY 15 registering a growth of 15 per cent over the previous fiscal, as demand in key markets such as the US and the UAE is on the rise. Apart from these traditional markets, markets in Eastern and Central European countries such as Poland also hold huge promise.

The Government of India in its Union Budget 2014-15, has provided investment allowance at the rate of 15 per cent to a manufacturing company that invests more than US$ 4.17 million in any year in new plant and machinery. The government has also taken steps to improve the quality of technical education in the engineering sector by allocating a sum of Rs 500 crore (US$ 78.8 million) for setting up five more IITs in the states of Jammu, Chhattisgarh, Goa, Andhra Pradesh and Kerala.

Ferro-manganese

Ferro-chrome

Ferro-silicon

Ferro-Nickel

Silico-manganese

For Setting Up Of New Projects Some Of The Thrust Areas Are

Mineral Based Industry

Iron & Steel

Cold Rolled Steel Ingots

Sponge Iron

Ferro Alloys

Aluminum
Fertilisers

Cement

Petrochemical & Downstream Industries

Blow Moulded Bottels & Jerry Cans

Disposable Syringes

Moulded House Ware Items

Plastic Ropes & Twines

HMHDPPE Bags

PP Thermoformed Disposable Products

Garbage Bags Projects

LD/LLDPE Wide Film Project

Paint Containers

Plastic Thermowares

Plastic Tarpulin

Tatami Mats

Mosquito & Fishing Net

Electronics & Information Technology

Assembly of audio-visual consumer products

Computer hardware and peripherals

Telecom equipment and user interfaces

Sub-assemblies and accessories of Telecom Equipment

Electronic fun and education toys

Consumables and electronic components, especially thos which require some form of design capability as an inheent part of the production cycle.

Metallurgical & Engineering

Manufacture of structural steel products such as M.S. rounds less than diameter, light sections of channels, angles and flats.

Manufacture of iron & steel furniture and other sheet metals such as safes, buckets, drums etc.

Manufacture of iron, brass and bell metal products such as gates, grills, postal seal and other foundry products.

Manufacture of different machinery items.

Manufacture of different Transport equipment.

Leather & Leather products

Lining leather from blue chrome E.I. skin rejection

Chrome up leather

Chrome football eather

Laminated leather

Gloving leather from sheep skins

Book binding leather

Fancy leather goods like marketing bags, suitcases, handbags, purses, presentation articles, waist belt, leather gloves & dress etc.

Manufacture of leather fur garments

Leather toys

Food & Agro Processing Industry

Fruit & Vegetable Processing

Pasta & Snack Food

Cereal, Pulses, Oil Seed Processing

Spices

Dairy & Milk Processing

Mushroom Cultivation & Processing

Fish Processing

Meat & Egg Processing

Medicinal Plant Extracts

Chemical Industry

Activated Carbon

Bromine

Caffeine

Calcium Carbonate

Casein

Citric Acid

Di-Methionine

Ferric Ox Of FerriteMagnetic grd.

Fused MagnesiaDead Burntmagnesite

L-Lysine-L-Lysine Hcl

Mannitol

Modified Starch

Mono Sodium Glutamate

Phytase

Poly Vinyl Alcohol

Potassium Carbonate

Potassium Chlorate

Sodium Chlorate

Strontium Carbonate

Titanium Dioxide

Vanillin

Vinyl Acetate Monomer

Gems & Jewelry

Tourism & Tourism related activities

Textiles & Geo textile

Jute Diversified Products

Woven geo textiles, Non woven geo textiles

Paving Products ,Silt Fences

Landscape and Erosion Control materials.

Carpet Backing Clothes

Food Grade Jute Bags, Hand & Shopping Bags

Handicrafts & Novelty Items, Home Furnishing Items

Hessian, Sacking, Yarn

Bio Technology

Therapeutic Proteins

Hybrid Seeds

Tissue Culture raised plants

Bio-fertilisers

Bio diversity conservation

Hydropower

Concentrating solar power plants

Solar thermal technologies

Wind Turbine Energy Projects

Geothermal Energy, Bio Mass Power

Government has keen interest to develop these(The red coloured) sectors. There is a big scope in these fields. In brief what to make can be summarized into the following category

AUTOMOBILE
AUTOMOBILE COMPONENTS
AVIATION
BIOTECHNOLOGY
CHEMICALS
CONSTRUCTION
DEFENCE MANUFACTURING
ELECTRICAL MACHINERY
ELECTRONIC SYSTEMS
FOOD PROCESSING
IT AND BPM
LEATHER
MEDIA AND ENTERTAINMENT
MINING
OIL AND GAS
PHARMACEUTICALS
PORTS AND SHIPPING
RAILWAYS
RENEWABLE ENERGY
ROADS AND HIGHWAYS
SPACE
TEXTILES AND GARMENTS
THERMAL POWER
TOURISM AND HOSPITALITY
WELLNESS

State wise priority sectors :

ANDHRA PRADESH

Food Processing, Software, Financial Services, Electronics, Petrochem, Power, Textiles & Tourism

ARUNACHAL PRADESH

Petrochem, Minerals, Agro-Processing, Oil & Natural Gas, Tourism & Power

BIHAR

Minerals, Engineering, Power, Telecom, Electronics, Consumer Durables, Plastics, Pharma, Leather & Leather Products.

CHATTISHGARH

Auto & Auto Components, Agricultural Implements, Minerals, White Goods, Telecom, Petrochem

DELHI

Restaurants, Tourism, Transportation, Power

GOA

Electronics, Marine Products, Mining, Tourism

GUJARAT

Garments, Gems & Jewellery, Food Processing, Leather, Ancillary Engineering Units

HARYANA

Agro Processing, Food Processing, Electronics, Tourism

HIMACHAL PRADESH

Agro Processing, Minerals, Tourism, Hydro Electric Power, Electronics

JHARKHAND

Minerals, Engineering, Power, Telecom, Electronics, Consumer Durables, Plastics, Pharma, Leather & Leather Products ,

JAMMU & KASHMIR

Food Processing, Handicrafts, Handlooms, Hotels, Fruit Based Industries, Restaurants, Tourism

KARNATAKA

Auto & Auto Ancillaries, Telecom, Electronics, Infotech, Agro Processing, Leather, Garments, Pharma

KERALA

Electronics, Mining, Food Processing, Tourism, Power, Shipping, Textiles

LADDAKH

Herbal Medicines, Ayurved Research centers, Horticulture Research Centers, Floriculture

MADHYA PRADESH

Auto & Auto Components, Agricultural Implements, Minerals, White Goods, Telecom, Petrochem

MAHARASHTRA

Electronics, Food Processing, Garments, Horticulture

MANIPUR

Agro Based Industries, Handicrafts, Petrochem, Electronics, Forest Based Industries, Minerals

MEGHALAYA

Agro Processing, Meat Processing, Forest Based Industries, Power, Minerals, Electronics & Infotech

MIZORAM

Agro Based Industries, Handlooms, Electronics, Sericulture, Handicrafts

NAGALAND

Agro Based Industries, Horticulture, Power, Handicraft, Tourism

ORISSA

Agro & Food Processing, Electronics, Telecom, Garments, Precision Engineering, Gem & Jewellery, Auto Parts

PONDICHERY

Electrical Equipment, Cement, Petrochem, Hotels & Restaurants, Services, Tourism, Transportation

PUNJAB

Agro Based Industries, Dairy Industries, Pharmaceuticals, White Goods Industries, Electronics, Tourism

RAJASTHAN

Agro Based Industries, Leather, Wool, Hotels, Ceramics, Tourism, Minerals

SIKKIM

Carpet Weaving, Commercial Cropping, Food processing, Hydroelectric Power, Tourism, Wool

TAMIL NADU

Auto & Auto Components, Pharma, Food Processing, Cement, Ceramics, Electrical Equipment

TELANGANA

Agro Based Industries, Agro Waste new products, Solar Energy, Plantations

TRIPURA

Agro Based Industries, Forest & Gas Based Industries, Handlooms, Handicrafts, Seriulture

UTTAR PRADESH AND UTTARAKHAND

Tourism, Agro Based Industries, Electronics, Sugar, Power Herbal Medicines, Ayurved Research centers, Horticulture Research Centers, Floriculture

WEST BENGAL

Petrochem, Iron & Steel, Engineering, Food Processing, Pharma, Mining, Tourism, Electronics & Infotech

Certain Fields are going to be opened up and certain projects are still unexplored . Refer to the Website link below for Computer Based New Generation Projects

https://www.elprocus.com/computer-science-projects-engineering-students/

https://ahduni.edu.in/seas/research/list-of-funded-projects

https://www.csir.res.in/rural-industry/2312

https://www.csir.res.in/rural-industry/2313

https://www.csir.res.in/rural-industry/2314

https://www.csir.res.in/rural-industry/2315

https://www.csir.res.in/rural-industry/2316

https://www.csir.res.in/rural-industry/2317

https://www.csir.res.in/csir-knowledgebase

Few guidelines we are collaborating here for your conven-
ience in selecting a Project keeping in consideration of its
location, category etc. If the promoter's thrust is basically
on the type/category of Project(as mentioned in point 1-3)
then how to arrive on one decision we are giving certain
case studies to be followed

If thrust is on 100% Export Oriented Units care must be
taken about the demand of your products in international
market , the quality of product (whether it is competitive
in), position of the Domestic Tariff Area(like distance of the
Domestic Market from your unit, market availability etc.).
To make the product competitive & qualitative it is better
to use foreign technologies; but the technologies should be
chosen such a way that there is no need to recruit foreign
technicians, engineers etc. as this would be very cost effective.

When thrust is given on export, it's better to avoid processing or production of perishable products in lack of refrig-
erated infrastructural facilities & locational disadvantages
like distance from the port. Further note if thrust is given
on the export of production & processing of perishable
products then unit should be set up in Export Processing
Zone to avoid all sort of procedural delays in shipping the
finished products as well as to get all sort of highly ad-
vanced infrastructural facilities.

Even if there is no thrust on Export but 100% thrust is on the production of a perishable item even then care to be taken to establish the unit very near to the urban area or cities or "A" class districts instead of curtailment of so many benefits of getting incentives. However such units could be established in the Industrial Parks like "FOOD PARKS" so that a promoter get a high weightage of quick sell and smooth and regularised buying of Raw material through NSICs.

Even if thrust is not on export the unit might be set up very near to the basic Raw Material sources if a specific basic Raw Material is a major input of any production item because in that case the processing cost, power cost, fuel cost, transportation cost as well as time will save which gives the ultimate economy of the production like the projects of "FERRO ALLOYS", "CHEMICALS", "PHARMACEUTICALS", "AGROBASED INDUSTRIES", "FORESTRY", "CHELLAC INDUSTRIES", "RUBBER/LATEX ITEMS" AND "ALL SORT OF NATURE BASED INDUSTRIES". Certain industries require a prominent marketing pattern instead of Raw Material sourcing due to availability of ready Raw Material in the urban/ city market. In such cases transportation & infrastructural facility becomes prominent and so such industry should be set up in Industrial Zone/ Industrial Parks/ Growth Centres near the urban market. Such industries are like "PRODUCTION OF CONSTRUCTION MATERIAL", "ALL SORTS OF PROCESSING, FABRICATING & ASSEMBLING INDUSTRIES", "ALL SORT OF CONSUMER INDUSTRIES" etc.

Even if thrust is on export then item is to be seen whether the transportation will be through water or air. If item is exportable by air then industry could be set up in any export promotion area like Export Promotional Industrial Park or may be in Industrial Town or Industrial Growth centres or Industrial Parks instead of going to the specific Export Processing Zone like FEPZ/ KEPZ/ SEPZ because more of these organised areas are near water & far distant from the urban area. Though the promoter will get all clearances at a single window but he will lack expertise qualified staff, skilled labour, urban infrastructural facilities to transport the products to different destinations which would be a big headache as well as cost effective for the promoter. So these facilities should be minutely studied and decided. This point becomes more important when a promoter plans to set up project like Polypropylene waste recycling industry, Stones & diamond processing, Garment manufacturing industry etc.

(B) There are certain cases where how thrust is given to select a category of Project in itself differs on financial, administrative and other factors like economies of scale etc...

If thrust is given on early return on total Capital Investment under circumstances like

If a production has complete threat of imported substitute due to import export liberalisation or WTO regime or due to any other Government policy then every investor would deserve to get back his net return on total investment as early as possible before the product get threat of rash competition or completely wiped out from the market due to more economy and cheap substitute from abroad or due to heavy advertisement by Multi National Companies (As for example Cosmetic range of products, Health care products, General consumer product, Electronic products etc.)

In such cases promoter should take care of   following points:- Besides various facilities, incentives in interior area industry must set up near urban areas and cities to get quick market. Promoter should take special care to develop his own "Brand", "Trademark", "Patents" of their product/ invention from the very initial stage.

Promoter must take care of export promotion probabilities from the very initial stage and should spread its wings from the neighbouring countries to the far countries.

Promoter must invest heavily on advertisement and make the product more marketable rather than to invest in high scale of manufacturing capacities or a big project.

Instead of going into the 100% EOU or the unit to be set up in Export Promoting Zone/Special Economic Zone the promoter should take care of setting up an Export Promotion Unit in Export Promotion Industrial Parks near urban areas to keep gates open from all around like a) Quick market in urban areas b) Smooth purchasing facilities c) Easy one point clearances d) Export probabilities

If a product has seasonal market for sale of finished product and/or for purchasing of Raw Material, like oil extraction industries/ agro/ horti/ forestry/ pisci/ flori based industries etc., every investor has to think twice to manage production, sale and profit most effectively and most early.

As we know once a season foregone another season will be caught up after a gap of several months which means cost factor of idle time, labor hour loss, machine hour loss, interest loss, more wear & tear of idle machinery.

Hence such industry should always be started with a small scale capacity with lower capacity plant and most gradually plough back the profit after investment in proper maintenance of the plant. Such industry if having product of perishable nature then extensive should be done on Refrigeration system. Incentives must be taken from the Government to reduce the burden of interest and to enjoy the working capital. Such industry should also be very near to the Raw Material sources(that's why generally rice bran oil industries are always set up very near to the rice producing areas), packaging should also be season proof, labour employment should also be on contractual basis even the financial record maintenance should also be on retainership/ contractual basis. Industry must have some facilities of producing some by products coming out from their Industry or the nearby industry to get minimum return n the off season to meet the fixed cost of operation of the unit.

If a product has such type of manufacturing facilities which get manufactured and operate economically on a specific scale only(like 5 MW furnace or 9 MW furnace in case of ferro alloys industry, 2 MT or 9 MT chilling plant in case of dairy industry etc..).

In such cases investor has very few options to select a particular scale of plant. He could choose only such plant which considering the fixed capital investment could be economically operated and give complete economy of scale(i.e IE a minimum percentage of profit as expected after meeting all expenses and interest on capital) where plants of low scale capacity if doesn't give marketable product to derive the minimum breakeven considering the fixed cost of establishing a unit, plants of high scale capacity get too costly to manage promoter's margin on institutional fund requisition. In case of lack of proper promoter's margin and fund to set up a reasonable scale of plant considering the minimum production and sale, profit and Break Even Point a promoter should avoid setting up these industries.

If a promoter's thrust is only on such industry on which he has long experience, technical knowledge due to his qualification, good marketing tie up probabilities with Indian and Foreign industries

Then a promoter most minutely detail out on papers each and every sector related to production, marketing, profit and break even for each scale of plants, its cost impact and fund arrangement together with market survey report, collaboration and buy back arrangement facility, External Commercial Borrowings at very cheaper, fund syndication probabilities of NRIs or collaborators etc.. Even after the minute calculation if a promoter is in confusion; how to mitigate the gap of scale of plant he must choose always on the conservative side for a lower scale of plant and properly planned for expansion of plant in next 2-3 years after getting a grip over the market by establishing their brand. Instead of thinking of ripping the profit in early years they must plan & organise the thing in a fashion to expand the unit first and to ripe the profit in long term.

However if thrust is on the quality of project having no problem of promoter's margin of fund as well as institutional fund then the promoter may take risk of getting up of long gestation period project (like Big infrastructural project, Import substituted project or the big collaboration project).

In such cases promoter should take a minute and detailed market survey report, detailed civil report, detailed technical reports, 10-15 years financial viability report, brand analysis report and all other technical inputs before going into the actual installation to avoid any sort of procedural or viability negativity. In such cases project may be collaboration projects with External Commercial Borrowings or NRI fund or Techno Equity Participation which are generally called Joint Ventures Such projects may be set up in any interior area to enjoy the backward district incentive and benefits as well as could develop economically backward regions to enjoy a vast space as well as Government support to develop that vast space. Emphasis should always be interior areas to get the vast land, cheap labor, cheap electricity, self modeled transportation facilities, self modeled communication & infrastructural facilities, good storage capacities etc

Even after proper analysis of all the points mentioned in category A and B above if promoter is still in mess to arrive on a conclusion then he must go through the following paragraph seriously In cases of numerous inputs one get naturally perplexed to derive a conclusion;

- He must categorized his priorities;
- He must write line of experience;
- He must study how closely & easily he can borrow technocrats/expertise of his priority project.
- He must analyze his complete fund availability
- He must bifurcate his fund into fixed & working capital fund then his fixed portion can at maximum be multiplied by 4 which will be his highest institutional fund requisition. Working Capital fund should be minimum 40% of the total fund available to the promoter. Then
- he must analyze banking loan of CC limit or Working Capital loan as 4 times of his own Working Capital margin.
- he should study what maximum interest free/ interest borne fund he could arrange from his friendly source.
- Now after analyzing complete fund availability/ requisition promoter should find whether project as per his priority/ experience easily available technology/expertise might be set up under the or with the above mentioned fund availability as in point (iv). If not omitting or matching then the promoter must give thrust on all the points mentioned in (v) Above and then start analyzing a few other project of his interest or ambition or as per **CURRENT MARKET TREND or CURRENT MARKET AVAILABILITY.**

After getting a preliminary product knowledge one should take detail knowledge through the Project related work, Trade fair, Joining seminar which held time to time, website if internet available or through consultants.

After selecting and getting information from a few project now the promoter should analyze what category/status should be better for the project whether Export Promotion Unit/ 100% Export Oriented Unit/ Simply Domestic Units/ Small Scale Industry/ Medium or Large Scale whatever.

Since location is a factor which must depends upon type and status of the project, category of the project, type of the project, type of product or as mentioned in case study of Category A or Category B the promoter's administrative facility.

[IF PROMOTER WILL FOLLOW THE ABOVE GUIDELINES/ FLOW CHART HE CAN EASILY FIXED ON A PARTICULAR PROJECT]

Where ?

where ?? The next step you have to take is to select places where you can set up your unit. For the New promoters "Land Identification" is a very crucial and difficult part .The different sectors of an economy are inter-dependent on each other. Industrial corridors, recognising this inter-dependence, offer effective integration between industry and infrastructure, leading to overall economic and social development.

Industrial corridors constitute world-class infrastructure, such as:

High-speed transportation network – rail and road

Ports with state-of-the-art cargo handling equipment

Modern airports, Special economic regions/industrial areas

Logistic parks/transshipment hubs, Knowledge parks focused on catering to industrial needs, Complementary infrastructure such as townships/real estate, Other urban infrastructure along with enabling policy framework

Five industrial corridor projects have been identified, planned & launched by the Government of India. These corridors are spread across India, with strategic focus on inclusive development to provide a boost to industrialization and planned urbanization. Manufacturing is a key economic driver in each of these projects. These projects are expected to play a critical role in raising the share of contribution of the manufacturing sector from approximately 16%[2] to 25% by 2025.

Smart cities are being developed along these corridors. These cities, with state-of-the-art infrastructure, will house the new workforce that is required to power manufacturing, in turn leading to planned urbanization.

DELHI-MUMBAI INDUSTRIAL CORRIDOR (DMIC)

The Delhi-Mumbai Industrial Corridor (DMIC) is a mega infrastructure project by the Government of India. The corridor covers an overall length of 1483 km between the political capital, Delhi, and the business capital, Mumbai, of India.

The US $100 bn project is being funded by the Government of India, Japanese loans, investments by Japanese firms and through Japan depository receipts issued by Indian companies.

Delhi Mumbai Industrial Corridor Development Corporation (DMIDC) is the incorporating agency for the project. DMIDC has been registered as a company with 49% equity of the Government of India, 26% equity of the Japan Bank for International Cooperation (JBIC) and the remaining held by government financial institutions. The DMIDC has been incorporated to establish, promote and facilitate the development of the DMIC project. It undertakes and assists project development services, for various central government agencies and state governments, relating to investment regions/industrial areas/economic regions/industrial nodes and townships.

Delhi Mumbai Industrial Corridor (DMIC) Project aims to create futuristic Industrial Cities by leveraging the "High Speed – High Capacity" connectivity backbone provided by the Western Dedicated Freight Corridor (DFC). [8]

The corridor will have 24 investment regions in eight manufacturing cities in Phase 1 of the project. [9] The five cities that have been chosen in Phase 1 as Investment Regions are

Manesar – Bawal (Haryana)

Dadri – NOIDA – Ghaziabad (Uttar Pradesh)

Ahmedabad – Dholera (Gujarat)

Pithampur – Dhar – Mhow (Madhya Pradesh)

Khushkhera – Bhiwadi – Neemrana (Rajasthan)

The three cities that have been chosen as Industrial Areas are

eas are

Shendra – Bidkin (Maharashtra)

Dighi Port (Maharashtra)

Jodhpur – Pali – Marwar (Rajasthan)

For more information please visit DMIDC Project Influence Area.

The DMIC Projects aims to achieve two goals: [11]

Triple industrial output in 9 years

Quadruple exports from the region in 8-9 years.

Current Status of Project:

The DMIC Project has made considerable progress with trunk infrastructure development activities nearing completion at four locations in Gujarat, Maharashtra, Uttar Pradesh and Madhya Pradesh. [12]

Developed land is being allotted to industries. 56 plots covering 335.51 acres of land area have already been allotted. This is expected to bring investments worth US$ 1.2 bn over a period of 3-5 years (as of December 2018). [13]

OTHER PROJECTS APPROVED BY DMIC TRUST ALONG WITH CURRENT STATUS OF THESE PROJECTS ARE AS UNDER:

Exhibition cum Convention Centre (ECC) in Dwarka

Cabinet has accorded its approval and Project Steering Committee has been constituted to steer the project.

M/s AECOM have been appointed as Program Management Consultants to take the various project developmental activities forward.

Airport Projects

Greenfield International Airport is being developed in Dholera in Gujarat. Land admeasuring 1426 Ha is in the possession of the State Govt. A SPV "Dholera International Airport Company Limited has been incorporated. No Objection received from Ministry of Defense and 'In principle' approval has been accorded by Ministry of Civil Aviation. Environment clearance has also been obtained from Ministry of Environment and Forests. M/s PWC has been appointed as the Transaction Advisor(s).

An Aerotropolis Project is also being developed as part of overall development plan of Khushkhera Bhiwadi Neemrana Investment Region in Rajasthan. The Techno – economic feasibility report has been prepared and has been approved by State Govt. Ministry of Defence has issued the No Objection Certificate for the Aerotropolis project in February 2015 and Site Clearance from Ministry of Civil Aviation (MoCA) has been received in November, 2015. The process for preparation of Detailed Project Report (DPR) has been initiated by DMICDC through Airport Authority of India (AAI).

Model Solar Project at Neemrana, Rajasthan

An SPV "DMICDC Neemrana Solar Power Limited" has been incorporated and equity has been released to the project SPV.

Lease deed has been executed and Power Purchase Agreement (PPA) for 5 MW plant executed between NTPC Vidyut Vyapar Nigam Ltd. (NVVN) & project SPV.

The project for 5MW has been commissioned as grid synchronization of 5MW Solar power plant is complete & power feeding to grid has commenced since 24th July, 2015. Commissioning Certificate has been issued by NTPC Vidyut Vyapar Nigam Ltd. (NVVN) on 3rd September, 2015.

PPA between M/s Mikuni India Pvt. Ltd., a Japanese company and M/s DMICDC NSPCL for 1MW has been executed.

Implementation Document (ID) has been executed between M/s DMICDC Limited and M/s Hitachi Limited.
Data Purchase Agreement between M/s Hitachi Limited and M/s DMICDC NSPCL for 1MW Solar has been executed.

DMICDC Logistics Data Services Project

The Shareholders' Agreement has been executed and project SPV by the name of "DMICDC Logistics Data Services" has been incorporated.

Port Operator Agreement has also been executed with Jawaharlala Nehru Port Trust (JNPT) on 17th February, 2016.

Operations have been initiated at JNPT Port with effect from 1st July, 2016.

750,000 containers have been tagged/de-tagged till 30th September, 2016.

Mass Rapid Transport System (MRTS) Projects

For the MRTS Project from Gurgaon to Bawal in Haryana, Final Detailed Project Report (DPR) has been submitted and approved by the State Govt. in February, 2016. The project is being included in JICA Special Rolling Plan for DMIC Project.

For MRTS Project between Ahmedabad to Dholera in Gujarat, final DPR has also been prepared and approved by State Govt. The project has also been included in the JICA Special Rolling Plan for DMIC Project in February, 2015.

Multi Modal Logistics Hub and Multi Modal Transport Hub, Dadri in Uttar Pradesh

The consultants are being appointed for preparation of Detailed Project Report (DPR).

State Govt. is under the process of acquiring land. Discussions have also been initiated with Dedicated Freight Corridor Corporation of India Limited (DFCCIL) so as to provide connectivity to the site from Western and Eastern Dedicated Freight Corridor.

AMRITSAR-KOLKATA INDUSTRIAL CORRIDOR (AKIC)

The Amritsar-Kolkata Industrial Corridor (AKIC) Project extends from Amritsar (Punjab) to Dankuni (West Bengal). The Eastern Dedicated Freight Corridor if the back bone of this economic corridor.[14] The AKIC covers six Indian states – Punjab, Haryana, Uttar Pradesh, Bihar, Jharkhand and West Bengal.[15] The length of the Amritsar-Kolkata Industrial Corridor (AKIC) is 1839 km across the six Indian states.[16]

The perspective planning of the AKIC has been completed and seven Integrated Manufacturing Clusters (IMCs) have been identified:[17]

The perspective planning of the AKIC has been completed and seven Integrated Manufacturing Clusters (IMCs) have been identified:[17]

Rajpura-Patiala (Punjab)

Prag-Khurpia Farms (Uttarakhand)

Bhaupur (Uttar Pradesh)

Gamhariya (Bihar)

Barhi (Jharkhand)

Raghunathpur (West Bengal)

Saha (Haryana)

The next step in the process if the development of the detailed master plan, preliminary designing and engineering for the areas that will be made available by the State Government.

BENGALURU-MUMBAI ECONOMIC CORRIDOR (BMEC)

The Bengaluru Mumbai Economic Corridor (BMEC) in intended to facilitate the development of a well-planned and resource-efficient industrial base served by world-class sustainable connectivity infrastructure, bringing significant benefits in terms of innovation, manufacturing, job creation and resource security.

The BMEC will be spread across Karnataka and Maharashtra.[18]he DMICD and the UK Trade and Investment (UKTI) have been determined as the nodal agencies on the Indian and UK sides respectively. DMICDC has appointed M/s Egis India Consulting Engineers Pvt. Ltd. in JV with IAU ile-de-France & CRISIL Risk & Infrastructure Solutions Limited as consultant for the feasibility study of BMEC.

CHENNAI-BENGALURU INDUSTRIAL CORRIDOR (CBIC)

The Chennai Bengaluru Industrial Corridor (CBIC) has been developed to achieve accelerated growth, regional industry agglomeration in the states of Tamil Nadu, Karnataka and Andhra Pradesh, and to facilitate the development of a well-planned and efficient industrial base.

The industrial corridor will achieve the goal by providing smooth access to industrial production units, reducing transportation logistic costs and improving delivery time as well as decreasing inventory cost. This will ensure increased private investments in manufacturing and industrial activity in the three states.

The Japan International Cooperation Agency (JICA) study team conducted a preliminary study for the Comprehensive Integrated Master Plan of the CBIC. The study team identified 25 priority projects, across various sectors, that aim to remove infrastructural bottlenecks in the project. The Mater Plan is spread over 20 years - 2013-2033.[19]

Delhi Mumbai Industrial Corridor Development Corporation (DMICDC) has been designated as nodal agency to take over the project work of the CBIC region. The Environment Impact Assessment (EIA) Consultants are being appointed by them for undertaking EIA studies.

Three nodes have been identified to be taken up for Master Planning:[20]

Tumkur (Karnataka)

Ponneri (Tamil Nadu)

Krishnapatnam (Andhra Pradesh)

VIZAG-CHENNAI INDUSTRIAL CORRIDOR (VCIC)

Vizag Chennai Industrial Corridor (VCIC) is the first coastal economic corridor in the country. It is part of the East Coast Economic Corridor (ECEC). [22]

It covers more than 800 km of Andhra Pradesh's coast-line and is aligned with the Golden Quadrilateral. [23] It also plays a critical role in the "Act East Policy" of India. The "Act East Policy" focuses on increasing the integration of the Indian economy with the economies of the Association of the Southeast Asian Nations (ASEAN). [24]

In September 2016, the Asian Development Bank (ADB) approved loans and grants worth US$ 631 mn[25] for the infrastructural development along the VCIC. The amount comprises.

"What is to be produced" also depends upon "Where is to be produced" and hence both the decisions should be made simultaneously.

To decide upon "Where is to be produced" again dependes upon so many sub factors like:-

Cost of the Land.

Recurring expenses on acquisition of land on lease or otherwise.

Nearby Market of the product & out sourcing facilities.

Density of population.

Nearby Market for Raw material availability.

Richness of area in term of production of Raw material

Infrastructural facilities like Power, Water, Communication, Transport.

Government Policies regarding Industries & Incentives effecting that area in particular.

Find out which is more suitable to the industrial unit- a city, suburban, rural or district location

If any particular climate suits your product, find out the area.

However sometimes project decision get very tough because of certain location disadvantages and sometimes get very easy due to location benefits and Govt. policies

Hence it is recommended to complete the Preliminary Task of Land Identification & Project Identification simultaneously and after summarizing all the inputs collected in this regard, should conclude its Survey and should decide a Specific Project to be set up at a Specific Location. Here we indicate some zones where you enjoy many sorts of facilities as well as Government's incentives, which help a lot to select a location.

EXPORT PROCESSING ZONE/FREE TRADE ZONE

Export Processing Zones have emerged as effective instruments to boost exports of manufactured products especially in developing countries. The Zones set up as enclaves separated from the Domestic Tariff Area by physical barriers are intended to provide an internationally competitive duty free environment for export production. This enables the product to be competitive both quality wise and cost wise in the International market

The EPZ/FTZ are as follows : -

Cochin Export Processing Zone, Kerala

Falta Export Processing Zone, West Bengal

Kandla Free Trade Zone, Gujarat

Madras Export Processing Zone, Madras

Noida Export Processing Zone, UP

Santacruz Electronics Export Processing Zone, Mumbai

Vishakhapatnam Export Processing Zone, Andhra Pradesh

Each zone provides basic infrastructural facilities, like developed land, standard design factory buildings, built up sheds, roads, power, water supply and drainage in addition to a whole range of fiscal incentives. Customs clearance facilities are offered within the Zone with no extra charge while facilities of Banking, Post offices, and clearing agents are also available in the Service Centres attached to each zone. In all EPZs multi product units are set up except in SEEPZ (Santacruz Electronics Export Processing Zone, Mumbai) which is confined to electronics and gems & jwellery.

Criteria for approval of project in a Zone:-
The unit should be 100% export oriented
Minimum Value Addition according to prescribed formula
Improvement in Industrial Technology
Export Marketing capability
Employment of skilled manpower
Process of manufacture should be pollution free.

EXPORT PERFORMANCE

Exports from EOU/EPZ units which stood at
Rs. 18,376.09 Crores in 2000-2001 rose to
Rs. 21,652.61 Crores in 2001-2002 representing a
growth of 17.83% Details of exports from EPZs/EOUs
during the last three years are indicated below:

Year	EPZs	EOUs	Total (Rs. In crores)
1999-	1776.69	13701.29	15477.98
2000-2001	2464.09	15912.00	18376.09
2001-	2917.61	18735.00	21652.61
2002-2003	1299.98	4396.92	5696.90(Apr-Sept'2002)

Special Economic Zones in the country is being developed
with a view to provide an internationally competitive and
hassle free environment for exports. Units may be set up
in SEZ for manufacture, trading, re-conditioning, and re-
pair or for service activity. The units in the Zone have to
be a net foreign exchange earner but they shall not be
subjected to any pre-determined value addition or minimum export performance requirements.

Sales in the Domestic Tariff Area by SEZ units shall be subject to positive foreign exchange earning and on payment of applicable Customs duty and import policy in force.

The followings are the Special Economic Zones as per the notice issued by the Government on 1.11.2000 on the basis of proposals received from the Private Sector/State Governments:

Positra (Gujarat)

Navi Mumbai and Khopta (Maharashtra)

Nanguneri (Tamil Nadu)

Kulpi and Salt Lake (West Bengal)

Paradeep and Gopalpur (Orissa)

Bhadohi,Kanpur,Greater Noida & Moradabad (U.P)

Vishakhapatnam and Kakinada (Andhra Pradesh)

Indore (Madhya Pradesh)

Hassan (Karnataka)

Vallarpadam/Puthuvypeen (Kerala)

The previously Export Processing Zones at Kandla and Surat (Gujarat), Santa Cruz (Maharashtra) and Cochin (Kerala) had also converted into Special Economic Zones.

SEZ Scheme

A designated duty free enclave & to be treated as foreign territory for trade operations and duties and tariffs.

The activities permitted to be carried out in the SEZs are manufacture of goods, services, production, processing, assembling, re-conditioning, re-engineering, packaging, trading etc.

SEZ units to be positive net foreign exchange earner within three years.

Duty free goods to be utilised over the approval period of 5 years.

Monitoring of performance of SEZ units by a committee headed by Development Commissioner and consisting of Customs.

EXPORT PERFORMANCE BY SEZ (Rs. In crores)	
Year	Amt.
2000-2001	6088.21
2001-2002	6271.94
2002-2003	6857.60

At present there are 370 units in operation in the four functional SEZs as on September, 2002.

INDUSTRIAL PARKS

Internationally, the current thinking is that a cluster of industrial units should be set up in a region so that they can share the same Infrastructural facilities and the cost of infrastructure per unit comes down. This makes the products in the market more competitive both quality wise & price wise as well as a particular industry get boosted. In line with this, our Government has promoted some specific industrial parks. Specific industries are being promoted in specific regions to derive location advantage.

Integrated Services

The "Industrial Park" offer several distinct advantages to the industry. It allows for grouping of similar industries in order that any peculiar requirements may be addressed through large common facilities. Being located away from large cities, the principal attraction of such facilities is that unlimited space becomes available for the establishment of large industrial units on virgin land at reasonable costs.

Economies of scale allow investments in common infrastructure facilities like housing, power, water supply, sewage treatment, communications, road links and security, which may not be available to individual industries.

Attracting Investments

It is noted that most domestic and multi-national corporations seeking to establish large industries in a country are establishing them at locations some distance away from the large cities, bringing tremendous development to these areas. Further sophisticated large scale industrial groups prefer a readymade facility provided by an industrial park as opposed to the hassles of land acquisition, obtaining of various approvals and interaction with a host of authorities.

The Central Government have so far approved 25 proposals for establishment of EPIPs in the States of Punjab, Haryana, Himachal Pradesh, Rajasthan, Karnataka, Kerala, Maharashtra, Tamil Nadu, Andhra Pradesh, Uttar Pradesh, Gujarat, Bihar, Jammu & Kashmir, Assam, Madhya Pradesh, West Bengal, Orissa, Meghalaya, Manipur, Nagaland, Mizoram and Tripura.

The EPIPs at Sitapura, Distt. Jaipur (Rajasthan), Bangalore (Karnataka), Ambarnath, Distt. Thane (Maharashtra), Surajpur, Distt. Gautambudh Nagar (U.P.), Gummidipoondi, Chengalpattu, Distt. MGR(Tamil Nadu), Amingaon near Guwahati (Assam), Kakkanad, Distt. Ernakulam (Kerala), Pashamylaram, Distt. Medak (Andhra Pradesh), Kundli, Distt. Sonipat (Haryana), Byrnihat, Distt. Ribhoi (Meghalaya) and Bhubaneswar, Distt. Khurda (Orissa) have been completed and allotment of space to large number of units have also been made in these EPIPs. Exports have already commenced from Karnataka, Rajasthan, Punjab, Haryana and Orissa EPIPs. The Parks in other States are at various stages of implementation.

INDUSTRIAL ESTATES

If the unit is not Export oriented then the easier and the convenient place for an industrial unit is the Industrial Estate. Governments have set up such estates numbering above 600 in urban, semi urban and backward areas. These estates have been developed not only to boost the industrial growth scenario but also the areas surrounding the estates. This is the reason why the Government provides more incentives and facilities to the unit set up in backward areas.

These estates have well planned factory accommodations in healthy environment with water, electricity and roads and conform to the rules and regulations laid down by the Factory Act. Besides common service facilities such as tool room, forging shops, foundries, electroplating units, heat treatment plants etc. are provided in many estates. Facilities like railway siding, banks, post and telegraph offices, telephones, showrooms for finished products etc. are also available. For ancillary unit Govt. has also developed many Industrial estates which are near the large industries. All sorts of infrastructural facilities like power, water, road etc. are available. For every industrial accommodation you should contact the Director of Industries of the state concerned.

GROWTH CENTRE

With a view to promote industrialization of backward areas in the country, the Government of India, in June, 1988, had announced the Growth Centre Scheme under which 71 Growth Centers were proposed to be set up throughout the country with basic infrastructure facilities such as power, water, telecommunications and banking to enable them to attract industries.

These have been allocated amongst States on the basis of combined criteria of area, population and extent of industrial backwardness. The Government of India has so far sanctioned 68 growth centers.

The Central Government assists the State Governments by contributing up to Rs. 1.0 millions by way of equity for each growth Centre. The balance funds are to be raised by the State Governments and their agencies, which implement the projects. The amount of Central assistance has been increased to Rs. 1.5 for each growth centre in the North-Eastern Region in view of the continued backwardness of the Region.

The total amount of Central assistance released under the Scheme since its inception is Rs. 31.671 millions (up to 31.12.2000).

The development of growth centers of each State is supervised by their Industrial Development Corporation.

Existing growth centers in West Bengal and its neighboring States: -

WEST BENGAL

RANINAGAR, DABGRAM, COOCHBEHAR, MALDA, BISH-NUPUR, KALYANI I, II & III, KHARAGPUR, ULUBERIA, FALTA, HALDIA I & II, JALPAIGURI, BOLEPUR, DURGAPUR, KHANYANI

ORISSA

BARGARH, JHARSUGUDA, DHENKANAL, KHURDA, ROURKELA, BHUBANESHWAR

JHARKHAND

ADITYAPUR, BOKARO, RANCHI, DUMKA, CHAIBASA, GODDA, DUMKA, KODERMA, NANKUM, TATISHRA, DHANBAD, JAMSHEDPUR

ASSAM

BARAPETA, GOALPARA, KAKOPATHAR, DULIAJAN, SARI-HAAJAN, LILABARI, MAIBONG, MAUJA, BALIPARA,

Why ?

~hy **???**

EXPORT PROCESSING ZONES

Facilities & Incentives: -

The Office of the Development Commissioner(DC) serves as
the one window office for all the units in the zone including customs, security and the Office of the Labor Commissioner of the State Government situated within the
Zone.

These zones offer a truly supportive environment by providing simplified procedures. This is especially so in the
clearance of matter relating to industrial approval, foreign collaborations etc. under a single window clearance
system. As for example for statutory clearances the Office of the DC provides assistance for obtaining of the
same from the concerned authorities . The office also
issues Certificate of Origin in respect of goods/services
of 100% EOUs issues, Import Export code and the Registration cum Membership Certificate of the concerned
Export Promotional Councils.

The DC is empowered to approve projects under an automatic approval scheme within no time with a view to ensure speedy implementation of projects where: -

Items do not attract compulsory licensing.

Where the location is in conformity with the prescribed parameters.

The units undertake to achieve exports and value addition norms as prescribed in the Export & Import policy in force.

The CIF value of imported capital goods is financed through foreign equity or foreign exchange required for import of plant & equipment (net of taxes) is within Rs. 100 Million and in case of import of second hand capital goods if an Import License is not required.

Where the unit is amenable to bonding by custom authority. The foreign technology agreement if any entered by the unit is restricted to a lump sum payment of 1 crore and 8% royalty (net of taxes) over a period of 5 years from the commencement of production.

The exports by the unit are to be physically made to the General Currency Area.

Incentives:-

- Entitled to sale/supply in the DTA linked to exports and subject to achievement of NFEP(Upto 50% of the FOB value of exports).

- Domestic suppliers of goods/services to such units also entitled to neutralisation/reversal and deferment of duty payable on such supplies.

- Ease of inter unit transfer of goods and services for processing/job working.

- Job working/domestic outsourcing to supplement in house capacity.

- Third party export

- Allows to work as a job worker for exports of DTA unit .
  Trading /Service activities/reprocessing/reconditioning/ Reengineering allowed.

- Ease of replacement of goods found defective/repair and maintenance etc. in the DTA.

- 100% EOUs can also freely deal in items, the import or export of which are otherwise canalized.

- Ease of disposal of scrap, wastes etc.

- Shift to operations under self-declaration and self certification.

- Exemption/Deferment of customs duty on import of Capital goods, Raw materials, Components, Consumables, Packaging material spares etc. provided they are not in the negative list of imports.

- Reversal of Local Level Taxes through reimbursement of Central Sales Tax.

- Exemption from payment of Sales Tax on purchase of local materials (In FEPZ, West Bengal)

- Foreign Equity up to 100% permitted. No restrictions o repatriation of capital remittance of profits & dividends.

- Clubbing of export (FOB value) made by the unit with that of other units of the parent company in the DT for grant of status such as EH/TH/STH/SSTH.

- Concession in the lease rent of industrial plots, Standard Design Factory (SDF) buildings or sheds allotted for the first three years.

- Exemption/deferment of Income Tax/Corporate Tax as per the Policy announced and regime applicable from time to time.

SPECIAL ECONOMIC ZONES

- **Facilities for SEZ Units**

- No license required for import.

- Duty free import of capital goods, raw materials, consumables, spares etc

- Duty free procurement of capital goods, raw materials, consumable spares etc. from the domestic market.

- 100% income-tax exemption for 5 years and 50% exemption for 2 years thereafter.

- Manufacturing, trading or service activity allowed.

- Domestic Sales on full Custom duty subject to import policy in force.

- No fixed wastage norms.

- Full freedom for subcontracting.

- Subcontracting of part of production permitted abroad.

- No routine examination by Customs of export and import cargo.

- Facility to realize and repatriate exports proceeds within 12 months.

- Re-export imported goods found defective, goods imported from foreign suppliers on loan basis etc. without G.R. waiver under intimation to the Development Commissioner.

- Facility to retain 100% of foreign exchange receipts in Export Earners Foreign Currency (EEFC) Account.

- 100% Foreign Direct Investment in manufacturing sector allowed through automatic route barring few sectors.

- Duty free import/procurement from Domestic Tariff Area (DTA) of goods for setting up of units in the Zone permitted.

- Exemption from service tax.

- Exemption from Central Sales Tax to sales made from domestic tariff area to SEZ units.

- Facility to set up offshore banking units in SEZs.

- 100% FDI to SEZ Franchisee for providing basic telephone service in SEZs.

- External commercial borrowing by SEZ units upto US $ 500 million in a year without any maturity restrictions through recognized banking channels.

Facilities for developer of SEZ

- Procure goods from the DTA without payment of duty or import goods duty free for the development, operation and maintenance of SEZ.

- Income-tax exemption for 10 years in first 15 years.

- Full freedom in allocation of developed plots to approved SEZ units on purely commercial basis.

- Full authority to provide services like water, electricity, security, restaurants, recreation centers etc. on commercial lines.

- Facility to develop township within the SEZ with residential areas, markets, play grounds, clubs, recreation centers etc. with 100% FDI.

- Exemption from Service Tax.

~hy ??? Choose India ?

Population of 1.31 billion out of which 767 million falls in the age group of 15-64 age group, and also set to become the youngest country with average age of 29 years by 2025

2nd largest Internet users base with 462 million Internet users.

India has demonstrable capability to reach near 100% literacy level by 2025

Considerable Upward mobility among all sections, more 150 million will be added to middle class by 2025 which will create Huge consumer market base of US$ 3.6 trillion by 2020 (BCG Report)

3rd largest economy in the world with size of US$ 8.6 trillion by purchasing power parity (PPP) and is expected to rise to US$ 20 trillion in size by 2025

Fastest growing economy in the world with the rate of 7.6% in 2015-16

India has an immediate investment opportunity of $1 trillion (Economic Times)

India enjoys stable/positive ratings from major credit rating agencies around the globe and has a total foreign exchange reserves of US$ 371 billion as on 30th Sep 16

2nd largest Railway Network in the world, used by 23 million travelers every day

2nd largest Road Network in the world stretching 3.3 million km

12 major ports, 200 notified minor and intermediate ports

Drive economic growth and improve the quality of life of citizens by enabling industrial and urban infrastructure development

INDUSTRIALIZATION AND URBANIZATION

- Industrial Corridors and 21 new nodal Industrial Cities to be developed:
- Delhi-Mumbai Industrial Corridor (DMIC)
- Chennai-Bengaluru Industrial Corridor (CBIC)
- Bengaluru-Mumbai Economic Corridor (BMEC)
- Vizag-Chennai Industrial Corridor (VCIC)
- Amritsar Kolkata Industrial Corridor (AKIC)

These 21 new nodal cities will be having advantages like; Large land parcels, Planned communities, ICT enabled infrastructure, Sustainable living, Excellent connectivity-Road, Rail etc.

Delhi-Mumbai Industrial Corridor is a mega infra-structure project of USD 100 billion with financial and technical aids from Japan, covering an overall length of 1,483 km. Dedicated Freight Corridor (DFC) of 1504 km as the backbone,

DMIC will intersect 7 states namely Delhi, Uttar Pradesh, Haryana, Rajasthan, Madhya Pradesh, Gujarat and Maharashtra

Doubling of Network of Roads by 2020 and Construction of 15,000 km new roads by 2017 is targeted under various projects

Railway projects such as Setting up of New Railway Stations, Modernization of Rolling stock, High Speed Railways, Port Mine connectivity etc. have been initiated for Modernizing and better connectivity of Indian Railways.

Eastern Dedicated Freight Corridor of 1840 km length and Western Dedicated Freight Corridor of 1504 km length is under construction as well as many projects are under planning stage.

Sagar Mala project is started by the Govt. of India to modernize India's Ports and Inland waterways so that port-led development can be augmented and coastlines can be developed to contribute in India's growth, providing a project outlay of US$ 10 billion

The Smart Cities Mission having a project outlay of US$ 7.69 billion is progressing, with Special Purpose Vehicles for 19 cities already set up.

Aviation industry with target of becoming 3rd largest by 2030 and to cater international and domestic traffic.

NEW DESIGN, INNOVATION AND R&D

Investment in innovation and R&D offers large payoffs in terms of economic growth and competitiveness in global economy

3rd largest tech driven Start-up ecosystem globally and Tech Startups in India are expected to reach 11,500 in 2020 from 4,300 in 2015

"Start-up India" initiative was launched aiming at fostering entrepreneurship and promoting innovation by creating an ecosystem that is conducive for growth of Start-ups.

Intellectual Property Rights Policy launched in May 2016 is having salient features:

Strong TRIPS compliant policy framework, Ease of Access using World-class IT enabled patent offices

Internationally acclaimed systems for International Searching and Preliminary Examination of patent applications

Augmentation of Manpower: 721 additional technically competent Patent Examiners appointed.

Time for examination of patents to come down to 18 months from 7 years by March, 2018

Time for examination of trademarks to come down to 1 month from 13 months by March, 2017

EASE OF DOING BUSINESS

Improved business processes and procedures open up new avenues of opportunities and create confidence among entrepreneurs as a result of which India moved up 12 places in the World Bank's Doing Business ranking 2016 released in October, 2015

Incorporation of a company reduced to 1 day instead of 10 days

Power connection provided within a mandated time frame of 15 days instead of 180 days

No. of documents for exports and imports reduced from 11 to 3

Validity of industrial license extended to 7 years from 3 years

Bankruptcy Code 2015 – New bankruptcy law, providing for simple and time-bound insolvency process to be operational by 2017

Goods and Services Tax – Single tax framework by April, 2017

Permanent Residency Status for foreign investors for 10 years

OTHER REFORMS

Online portals for Employees State Insurance Corporation (ESIC) and Employees Provident Fund Organization (EPFO) for Real-time registration

Payments through 56 accredited banks

Online application process for environmental and forest clearances

Department of Commerce, Government of India has launched Indian Trade Portal. Important feature of this portal is to be a single point for relevant information on measures other than tariff called the non-tariff measures like standards, technical regulations, conformity assessment procedures, sanitary and Phytosanitary measures which may affect trade adversely.

An Investor Facilitation Cell has been created in 'Invest India' to guide, assist and handhold investors during the entire life-cycle of the business.

The Department of Industrial Policy and Promotion has also set up Japan Plus and Korea Plus. They are special management teams to facilitate and fast track investment proposals from Japan and South Korea respectively.

MAJOR FDI REFORMS

FDI stimulates country's economic development and creates more conducive environment for the industry to grow

Defence: Up to 49% under automatic route and above 49% through Government route

Civil Aviation: 100% FDI under automatic route in Greenfield Projects and 74% FDI in Brownfield Projects under automatic route beyond 74% for Brownfield Projects is under government route.

Broadcasting: New sectoral caps and entry routes are as under:

Broadcasting Carriage Services & down-linking of news channels: 100% FDI

Cable Networks: 100% FDI and in News channels: 49% FDI

Banking: FDI up to 74% with 49% under automatic route rest through government route

Railways: 100% FDI under automatic route permitted in construction, operation and maintenance of Rail Infrastructure projects

Construction: 100% FDI through automatic route and Removal of minimum floor area & minimum capital requirement

Pharmaceuticals: The extant FDI policy on pharmaceutical sector provides for 100% FDI under automatic route in Greenfield pharma and FDI up to 74% under automatic route and 100% under government approval in Brownfield pharma.

Plantation: Certain plantation activities namely; coffee, rubber, cardamom, palm oil tree and olive oil tree plantations has opened for 100% foreign investment under automatic route.

Telecom: FDI up to 100% with 49% under automatic route

Insurance & Pension: FDI Policy has been reviewed to increase the sectoral cap of foreign investment from 26% to 49% with foreign investment up to 26% to be under automatic route.

Medical Devices: 100% FDI under automatic route for manufacturing of medical devices has been permitted.

E-Commerce: 100% FDI in B2B e-commerce, Single brand retail trading entity permitted for B2C e-commerce and e-commerce food retailing

Retail: 100% FDI and 49% under automatic route is allowed. In case of 'state-of-art' and 'cutting-edge technology' sourcing norms can be relaxed subject to Government approval.

100% FDI is now permitted under automatic route in Duty Free Shops located and operated in the Customs bonded areas.

The Ease of Doing Business

The Ease of Doing Business (EoDB) index is a ranking system established by the World Bank Group. In the EODB index, 'higher rankings' (a lower numerical value) indicate better, usually simpler, regulations for businesses and stronger protections of property rights.

The research presents data for 190[1] economies and aggregates information from 10 areas of business regulation:

Starting a Business

Dealing with Construction Permits

Getting Electricity

Registering Property

Getting Credit

Protecting Minority Investors

Paying Taxes

Trading across Borders

Enforcing Contracts

Resolving Insolvency

INDIA – EASE OF DOING BUSINESS RANKING

Among the chosen 190[2] countries, India ranked 77th in 2018 in the World Bank's Doing Business index. Since then, various new reforms are underway, ushering remarkable improvement. In 2014, the Government of India launched an ambitious program of regulatory reforms aimed at making it easier to do business in India. The program represents a great deal of effort to create a more business -friendly environment.

The efforts have yielded substantial results with India jumping 65 places in the Doing Business rankings since 2014.

Positive changes have led to this impressive improvement in India's ranking in the EoDB index. India's major achievement is summarized here:

Construction Permits: India's ranking on this parameter has improved from 184 in 2014 to 52 in 2018.[4] This improvement has been mainly on the account of a decrease in the number of procedures and time taken for obtaining construction permits in India.[5]

Getting Electricity: India's ranking on this parameter has improved from 137 in 2014 to 24 in 2018. The number of days taken to get an electricity connection for a business is just 55 days and it takes only 3.5 procedures in Delhi Mumbai combined.[6]

Apart from these significant improvements, among the 190 economies, India ranks 7th in Protecting Minority Investors and 22nd in Getting Credit.[7]

The Ease Of Starting a Business

Permanent Account Number (PAN), Tax Deduction & Collection Account Number (TAN), Director Identification Number (DIN) have now been merged into a single form (SPICe) for company incorporation.[8]

Five-page form and other attachments for reserving the name of the Company with the Ministry of Corporate Affairs has been simplified into a simple web service with only three fields to be filled.[9]

Registration under Employee State Insurance Corporation (ESIC) and Employee Provident Fund Organisation (EPFO) are available at Shram Suvidha portal as a common online service with no physical touch point.[10]

No requirement of inspection for before registration under Shops & Establishment Act in Mumbai and Delhi. [11]

Companies Act was amended to eliminate the requirement of a common company seal. [12]

DEALING WITH CONSTRUCTION PERMITS

Municipal Corporations of Delhi, as well as Municipal Corporation of Greater Mumbai, have introduced fast track approval system for issuing building permits with features such as Common Application Form (CAF), provision of using digital signature and online scrutiny of building plans.

Delhi has uniform building by-laws which allow for risk-based classification regimes for different building types. It has a provision of deemed approval of sanctioning building plans within 30 days.

For construction permits, the time reduced from 128.5 to 99 days in Mumbai and from 157.5 to 91 days in Delhi between Doing Business 2018 and 2019 reports. [13]

Total number of procedures reduced to 20 in Mumbai and 16 in Delhi. Cost of obtaining construction permits reduced from 23.2% to 5.4% of the economy's per capita income. [15]

TRADING ACROSS BORDERS

The Central Board of Excise and Customs (CBEC) has implemented 'Indian Customs Single Window Project' to facilitate trade. Importers and exporters can electronically lodge their customs clearance documents at a single point. The number of mandatory documents required for customs purposes, for both import and export of goods, has been reduced to three.

e-Sanchit, an online application system, allows traders to file all documents electronically.

The electronic self-sealing of the container at the factory has reduced time and cost for exporting firms.

A computerized risk management system has brought transparency and reduced frequency of custom inspections significantly.

Central Board of Indirect Taxes and Customs has provided a facility for Advance Bill of Entry (Advance Import Declaration).

ENFORCING CONTRACTS

The Commercial Courts and Appellate Division of High Courts have been established in Mumbai and Delhi.

National Judicial Data Grid (NJDG), provides case data including case registration, cause list, case status and orders/ judgements of courts district-wise across the country. NJDG is open for public since 2015.

New cases in district courts are assigned to Judges randomly through an automated system in Delhi and Mumbai.

e-filing of cases has been introduced in district courts of Delhi and Mumbai.[21] 5. A case management tool has been developed with functionality of sending a notification to lawyers, viewing court orders/ judgements, tracking the status of cases, to semi-automatically generate court orders etc.

GETTING CREDIT

Central Registry of Securitization Asset Reconstruction and Security Interest (CERSAI) is a geographically unified electronic registry that provides for registration by asset type. Since 2017, CERSAI also provides search through debtor's name.

Securitization and Reconstruction of Financial Assets and Enforcement of Security Interest (SARFAESI) (Central Registry) Rules, 2011 was amended to include additional types of charges, including a security interest in - immovable property by the mortgage, hypothecation of plant and machinery, stocks, debt including book debt or receivables, intangible assets, patent, copyright, trademark, under-construction building.

The definition of property, which now includes immovable as well as intangible, allows CERSAI to register these additional charges. [25]

GETTING ELECTRICITY

Electricity connection is provided within 7 days if no Right of Way (RoW) is required and within 15 days where RoW is required.

Service line cum Development charges is now capped at US$ 357.6 in Delhi.

Number of documents required for getting electricity connection has been reduced to two and no physical documents are accepted.

Total number of procedures reduced to 3 in Delhi and 4 in Mumbai.

REGISTERING PROPERTY

All sub-registrar offices have been digitized and its records have been integrated with the Land Records Department, in both Delhi and Mumbai.

In Mumbai, all property tax records have been digitized. Property is mutated at automatically after registration.[30] The digitization of property records ensures transparency and allows citizens to ascertain the history of transactions in digital mode.

Online service for charges search at Registrar of Companies reduces the time taken for this procedure significantly.

Statistics regarding the number of land disputes at Revenue Courts are available online in both Delhi and Mumbai.

PAYING TAXES

Reduction of corporate tax from 30% to 25% for mid-sized companies.

Robust IT infrastructure of online return filing for Indian taxpayers.

The Goods and Service Tax came into effect from 01 July 2017. It subsumes eight taxes at the Central and nine taxes at the State level.

The Employee State Insurance Corporation (ESIC) has developed a fully online module for electronic return filing with online payment. This has substantially reduced the time to prepare and file returns.

With the introduction of the e-verification system, there remains no physical touch point for document submission to income tax authorities.

RESOLVING INSOLVENCY

The Insolvency and Bankruptcy Code of 2016 has introduced new dimensions in resolving insolvency in India. It is India's first comprehensive legislation of corporate insolvency.[33]

Under Fast-track Corporate Insolvency Resolution Process (CIRP) for mid-sized companies, the process for insolvency shall be completed within 90 days with a maximum grace period of another 45 days.

MEASURES UNDERWAY

Paying Taxes: GST implementation.

Resolving Insolvency: Increased usage of Fast-track Corporate Insolvency Resolution Process (CIRP) as more insolvent companies opt for reorganization plans instead of liquidation.

Enforcing Contracts: Faster resolution of commercial disputes through dedicated commercial courts.[40] Registering Property: Digitization of land records and maps will bring transparency on encumbrances and ease the process of registering property.

Many State Level Reforms

Department for Promotion of Industry and Internal Trade (DPIIT) launched Business Reforms Action Plan (BRAP) and its assessment report in September 2015, capturing the findings of reforms implemented by States/Union Territories.

In 2016, DPIIT released a 340-point BRAP. It included recommendations on 58 regulatory processes and policies spread across ten reform areas spanning the lifecycle of a typical business.

BRAP 2017-18 was updated to 372 action points. It included new sectors such as Healthcare and Hospitality, Central Inspection system, Trade License, Registration under Legal Metrology, and Registration of Partnership Firms & Societies.

Assessment for BRAP 2017-18 included feedback score which was sought on 78 reform points from actual users. For BRAP 2019, DPIIT has proposed to undertake a 100% feedback based assessment. The reform areas included. [42]

Access to Information and Transparency Enabler

Single window system

Land administration and Transfer of Land and Property

Land availability and allotment

Environment Registration Enablers

Construction Permit Enablers

Labour Regulation-Enablers

Obtaining Utility Permits

Paying Taxes

Inspection Enablers

Contract Enforcement

Sector Specific: Healthcare and Miscellaneous

Detailed information on ease of doing business measures

implemented by various states is available at

http://eodb.dipp.gov.in.

Pradhan Mantri MUDRA Yojana (PMMY)

Pradhan Mantri MUDRA Yojana (PMMY) is a scheme launched by the Hon'ble Prime Minister on April 8, 2015 for providing loans up to 10 lakh to the non-corporate, non-farm small/micro enterprises. These loans are classified as MUDRA loans under PMMY. These loans are given by Commercial Banks, RRBs, Small Finance Banks, MFIs and NBFCs. The borrower can approach any of the lending institutions mentioned above or can apply online through this portal www.udyamimitra.in . Under the aegis of PMMY, MUDRA has created three products namely 'Shishu', 'Kishore' and 'Tarun' to signify the stage of growth / development and funding needs of the beneficiary micro unit / entrepreneur and also provide a reference point for the next phase of graduation / growth.